BLESSED ARE YOU WHO BELIEVED

BLESSED ARE YOU WHO BELIEVED

CARLO CARRETTO

Translated by Barbara Wall

BURNS & OATES
———
VERITAS PUBLICATIONS

First published in Great Britain 1982
by Burns & Oates Ltd
Wellwood, North Farm Road
Tunbridge Wells, Kent, TN2 3DR

in association with

Veritas Publications
7/8 Lower Abbey Street
Dublin, 1

Reprinted 1984

Originally published 1980
under the title *Beata te che hai creduto*
by Edizioni Paoline, Rome
© Edizioni Paoline, Roma, 1980
English translation © Search Press 1982
ISBN   (UK) 0 86012 129 1
        (Ire) 0 86217 068 0

Printed and bound in Great Britain by
Biddles Ltd, Guildford, Surrey

Typeset by Inforum Ltd, Portsmouth

CONTENTS

BLESSED ARE YOU WHO BELIEVED

1

THE MADONNA OF THE LITTLE TRUCK

Brother!

Sister!

Before you start reading this book, take a look at the picture on the cover. You will find there something rather odd.

The infant sitting on the Madonna's knee is clasping a little truck instead of the bird originally placed in his hand by the anonymous fifteenth-century painter – a little truck that might have been carved by St Joseph from some left-over piece of wood.

I am responsible for this substitution and I shall explain why.

I was thirty-six years old when Pope Pius XII summoned me to Rome to direct Catholic Action for young people. This was no mean task. Since that time this Catholic movement has spread out into myriads of rivulets, but then there was just one single organisation consisting of about half a million young people, fourteen publications, and over 20,000 associated groups.

I often felt crushed by the sheer weight of my responsibilities, especially when I travelled into Rome from the suburbs.

Yes, Rome was my agony, for the work was beyond my strength. Indeed the sight of those ancient stones exuding their indescribable mystery, and of St Peter's Square which, to the tourist, spoke of nothing but sweetness and light, caused me such acute suffering that sometimes I felt almost paralysed.

At home I had a copy of the famous picture on the cover. I treasured it because I loved it and because it spoke of dear and tender things.

I don't quite know how it happened; I only know that one

day I felt impelled to pick up my paint-brush and replace the bird with the little truck that symbolised my family name.*

Doing this made me feel as if I was communing with Mary, as if I was saying to her, 'Now, watch out; I am happy to be a toy truck in your son's hands, especially now when things are hard; but watch out!'

The agony of Rome did not entirely leave me, but what is certain is that when I felt myself getting tense it helped me to stay calm if I saw myself as part of that peaceful picture.

I can truthfully say that whenever I was in difficulties my thoughts flew to that picture of Jesus holding his little wooden truck, the image of another little truck trundling around the dusty roads of the world.

I must admit, however, that my relations with Mary, the mother of Jesus, were somewhat marred by the romanticism of the type of Marian devotion that was all the rage before the Vatican Council and which gradually became empty of meaning.

Mary as a queen to end all queens, Mary as a creature who could do no wrong, who walked about the streets of her Nazareth with a totally clear vision of things, incapable of sin or doubt – this Mary had little to say to anguished people trailing laboriously around in a wilderness of faith.

The exaltation of Mary through the enthusiasm of fanatics (so numerous in the Catholic world) ends by emptying our devotion to her of authentic theological content. She is, after all, the mother of God and has no need of recommendation to be esteemed. Better not betray the Gospel.

So it has not surprised me to observe the springs of love for Mary of Nazareth drying up in these past years among the young, nor to see the sellers of rosaries shutting up shop.

It was necessary for this to happen.

As with many other things, we had to start again from the beginning.

Have we not started again from the beginning with the Old Testament which in my country was regarded when I was young as a forbidden book?

Have we not started again from the beginning with the

Carretto, in Italian, means a little cart or truck.

liturgy which, before the Council, was expressed with cold restricted gestures and in a language, Latin, that the masses could not understand?

Have we not started again from the beginning with the Church which in the past was viewed as a clerical pyramid, whereas the Council has now described it as 'the people of God' making its way towards the Promised Land?

So let us also start again from the beginning with Mary, even if 'starting from the beginning' is only an illusion – because in reality things continue, because in the Church, which is a living body and a living reality, everything is continuous.

For myself, this beginning-again was an important moment in my life.

It occurred during my long period in the desert.

I was living in the Hoggar in a fraternity of the Little Brothers of Charles de Foucauld, and I was earning my bread by working as a meteorologist in the region of Tit, Tazruk and In Amguel. I enjoyed the work not only because it provided me with food but because it gave me the opportunity to live in the place of my choice, namely the desert, and to unite my daily task with its huge silences and the possibility of prolonged prayer.

Before long I got to know the Tuaregs who lived in tents, the Aratini who cultivated the oases, the Arabs who came from the north, and the Mozabites who specialised in commerce.

I was particularly fond of the Tuaregs whose tents were pitched along the *guelta*, a rocky basin where water surfaces, and on the uplands; and as I journeyed I often stayed with them in the evenings after my work.

It was during an encounter of this kind that I became aware of an interesting fact.

Quite by chance I discovered that a girl in the camp where I was staying was betrothed to a boy in another camp, but she hadn't yet gone to live with him because he was too young. I could not help linking this piece of information with that passage in the Gospel where it says that the Virgin Mary was betrothed to Joseph but they had not yet come together (Mt 1,18).

3

Two years later I went back to that camp and, looking for a topic for conversation, asked if the marriage had yet taken place. There was a look of embarrassment on my inter-locutor's face followed by an awkward silence.

So I did not pursue the subject. But later that evening, when I went to draw water at the *guelta* about a hundred metres from the camp, I fell in with one of the chief's servants and asked him the meaning of the awkward silence.

The servant looked cautiously around; then, because he trusted me as being a *marabout** he made a sign that I knew well – he passed his hand under his chin in a gesture characteristic of the Arabs when they want to convey that someone has had his or her throat cut.

The reason?

Before the wedding it was discovered that the girl was pregnant and the honour of the betrayed family required this sacrifice.

A shiver went down my spine to think that the girl had been killed because she had not been faithful to her future husband.†

That evening at compline, beneath the Sahara sky, I read Matthew's account of the conception of Jesus. I had to light a candle because it was a dark moonless night. I read: 'When his mother Mary had been betrothed to Joseph, before they came together she was found to be with child of the Holy Spirit; and her husband Joseph, being a just man and unwilling to put her to shame, resolved to send her away quietly.' (Mt 1,18/19).‡

So Joseph had not denounced her, nor had her father, Joachim, assumed the role of Khomeini and killed her as the law decreed – 'Moses commanded us to stone such' (Jn 8,4).

I remember vividly how it was on that evening. I felt that Mary was very close, squatting on the sand, small, weak, defenceless, with her large belly, unable to lean forward, silent.

---

*A man of God, in Islamic terminology

†Our surprise at these facts about the execution of adulterers is due to our ignorance of history. The defence of matrimonial chastity on the part of society has been appallingly strict in the past. Moses himself laid down that offenders of this kind should be killed (cf Deut. 22,24; Jn 8,4). Khomeini in Iran horrifies us today with his socio-religious policy when he orders adulteresses to be shot. He in fact is simply looking to the past when the law punished adultery in a similar way. Islam, which has not had a Jesus to temper laws with compassion, is always looking back to the primitive intransigence of the law.

‡The biblical quotations throughout this book are taken from RSV.

I put out the candle.

But I saw shining eyes all around me, eyes like jackals' eyes when they are waiting for little lambs.

They were the eyes of the inhabitants of Nazareth spying on the girl-mother and asking her with all the force of incredulity that men, and still more women, are capable of: 'What have you done to have that child, you dissolute wretch, you slut!'

What a night!

What could I answer?

That God is the baby's father?

Who would believe me?

I said nothing.

God knows.

God provides.

Poor gentle Mary, poor little girl-mother. What a bad start to your life!

How are you going to face so many enemies, and who will believe you?

That evening I felt for the very first time that I was getting somewhere near to the mystery of Mary.

For the first time I saw her not as a static statue on an altar, robed like a queen, but as a sister here beside me, seated on the sand of the world, her sandals threadbare like mine and with exhaustion in her heart.

Then I understood why her cousin Elizabeth, whom Mary visited after all these happenings (one is always very ready to leave one's own surroundings when one is big with child and the object of neighbours' puritanical scrutiny) – why her cousin Elizabeth said to her after hearing her story:

'Blessed are you who believed.'

Yes, truly blessed!

Mary, we need courage to believe all these things!

It is difficult for us to believe what you say when you tell us that your child is not the result of some nocturnal adventure that you do not wish to dwell on.

But above all it is difficult for you.

'Blessed are you who believed' (Lk 1,45).

It is the least that can be said to a poor, simple, humble girl who has had the experience of speaking with angels – she who is a no-one – and who has been told that she shall have a son who will be the Holy One and the son of the Most High – yes, she, the last and least of the 'remnant' of Israel.

'Blessed are you who believed, Mary.'

It was that evening on the sand, near the *guelta* of Issakaras-sem, that I decided to choose Mary as my instructor in the faith.

I had discovered a vital contact with her. She was no longer a remote figure to whom I owed 'worship', she was the sister of my heart, the companion of my pilgrimage, my teacher in the faith.

Yes, in my very faith.

Let me explain. Let me tell you, my brothers and sisters, that I have made the whole pilgrimage of faith, and I have made it on foot.

My good fortune has been that I have not trembled in the dark nor slackened my pace even at my last gasp.

My years in the desert have been a great help to me even though it was there that I experienced the 'dark night' described by St John of the Cross.

Now I feel I am the brother of all who call themselves atheists (and there are not many of them) and still more of all who have difficulty in believing and do not yet understand the real terms of the problem (and of these there are many).

If you come to my grave when I am dead (and I hope this will be soon for I have known our Lord and long to see his face) and if you believe that communication between members of the Kingdom is possible, don't ask me to pray that this or that ill of yours may be cured. Ask me one thing only, to pray for your faith.

It is the only gift that merits prayer.

And then if I can do it I shall do it. I shall look in silence into the eyes of Mary of Nazareth and try to draw what you need from the contemplation of her who had such courage in belief.

Brothers and sisters, I have opened my heart to you, I have told you everything.

Now if you are listening to me get your rosary and put it in your pocket. It may be years before you say it properly. That doesn't matter, keep it near you.

It will help you. Even if, when you slip it through your fingers, you say no more than: Hail Mary.

2

HAIL MARY

After I had been told that the girl-mother in the Tuareg encampment had been killed because she was caught in adultery, my relations with Mary of Nazareth became much closer.

It was as if she suddenly became my sister. I was not used to seeing her so human, so frail, so near to me. The liturgy had fostered a supernatural relationship, yes, but it had stifled Mary's voice as a woman, a creature, a sister, a teacher – a voice which just beside me could say so much more to me.

Yes, I must humbly admit it. It was not until I saw that silent tragedy of the Tuareg encampment in the light of Luke's Gospel that I fully understood Mary's courage in accepting what the angel told her about God's plans for her.

She had to accept the role of a girl-mother.

And who was going to believe her? If a young girl had come to my home in Piedmont and said, 'But I assure you, this baby I'm carrying is the son of the Most High,' no one would have believed her.

In my home my father would certainly have given her a slap in the face, and that was Piedmont. Further south she would have been told to get out – 'we don't want to see you ever again, you've disgraced the family'.

In an Arab or Scythian or Jewish family in past times, blood would have flowed.

Mary had the courage to trust in the God of the impossible and to leave the solution of her problems to him. Hers was pure faith.

We must not forget that the Bible was written precisely in that region between the desert and the steppe where there are wandering caravans, where sheep and asses graze, where men know how to question the sky because it is their only hope of life.

And I was there too. When at night I set up camp at the side of the track and lit the fire to bake the bread and boil the tea, Mary came and joined me. I had only to bring out my rosary which I myself had made (its beads were cut from wood collected in Issakarassem) and which I always carried in my pocket, to feel Mary's presence beside the fire. The desert is a huge church with the starry sky as the vault and the fine hot sand as the mat on which to sit and pray.

What pleasure to forget the notion of time and space and live the communion of saints as a tender reality.

It was for this that I came to the desert. I longed to break the barrier between the visible and the invisible, between the sky and the earth, and in faith I often succeeded.

What peace to penetrate beyond the world of things! To live as if the Gospel was being written now, being lived now.

To see the symbol of God as manifested in things fading away and revealing his invisible presence, his divine reality.

To be able to speak with the saints.

To experience the eucharistic presence within my tent which was transformed into a tabernacle.

One evening I tried to talk to Mary.

It was so easy!

I loved her so much!

Mary, tell me how it all happened. Tell me everything as you told it to Luke for his Gospel.

You know it all, she said, because you know the Gospel.

It was very wonderful.

I was living in Nazareth in Galilee and my life was the life of all simple girls – work, prayer, poverty, great poverty, but joy too, and above all hope in the destiny of Israel.

I lived with Anna, my mother, in a simple little house with a courtyard in front surrounded by a wall built on purpose so that we women could live in freedom and privacy.

I often went there to work and pray. I felt these activities to be intimately linked and I was full of peace and joy.

That day I was alone in the small courtyard and suddenly I was bathed in light.

I was sitting on a stool, praying. My eyes were half-closed and I felt a great joy invading my whole being.

The light got brighter and I began to open my eyes which I had closed so as not to be dazzled.

I was happy to let myself be filled by that radiance. It seemed a sign of God's presence enfolding me like a cloak. Suddenly the light took on the shape of an angel. I have always imagined angels like that, just as he appeared to me then.

You know about the problem of faith. You're never certain if the vision is within or without.

It is certainly within because if it was only without then you would suspect that it was an illusion, that you were 'seeing things'.

But within there is no such thing as illusion. It just *is* like this, you *know* it is like this, and God is your witness.

I sat very still for fear that everything would vanish.

But instead of the angel vanishing, he spoke. Here, too, you do not quite know whether you hear the voice in your ear or deep inside you.

Certainly inside you, because if you heard it only outside in your ear then it could be an illusion.

I heard the voice there where God himself is my witness.

And what did it say?

It said: Hail Mary, full of grace, the Lord is with you.

And what did you feel?

I was naturally very worried. It was as if I was being visited by things too immense for me and for my smallness. You can think about the things of God with great yearning, but when they touch you you can't help being afraid.

And indeed the first thing the angel said was:

'Do not be afraid, Mary' (Lk 1,30).

This gave me courage because I had heard that very phrase in the synagogue when they read the story of Abraham:

'Fear not, Abram, I am your shield' (Gen. 15,1).

Then the angel announced my motherhood. His words were few but so stark and clear that I felt they were springing up within me. Never before had it happened to me to hear words as if they were great events.

Tell me, Mary, were you surprised? Had it ever occurred to you that you, even you. . . .?

Yes, of course it had occurred to me. We Jewish girls hardly thought of anything else. We felt that the time had come, and when we prayed in the synagogue the air was heavy with expectation of the Messiah.

What did you understand when the angel told you that you were the chosen one and that the Messiah would be born from you?

I understood exactly what he was saying, yet I was amazed by the strangeness of it, for how was it possible if I was a virgin?

The angel explained and it was easy to accept what he said, for I felt I was immersed in God as in that brilliant noonday light.

I even confusedly foresaw all the misunderstandings there would be, how I wouldn't be able to explain things to my mother and still less to my fiancé Joseph, but I couldn't have stopped myself, so strong was God's hold on me and so strong was the conviction that came from the angel's words:

'For with God nothing will be impossible

'For with God nothing will be impossible

'For with God nothing will be impossible' (Lk 1,37).

Gradually the light faded and the angel disappeared from my sight.

I saw my mother Anna crossing the courtyard and I wanted to tell her what had happened, but I couldn't, because I couldn't find the right words.

Then I realised that there were no words with which I could explain what had happened.

So as the days passed the more silent I became.

Talking to my fiancé Joseph was even more difficult.

You know what the custom was in our tribe. A girl was betrothed very early. It was like an arrangement between families.

But as the future bride was so young she went on living with her family until she was ready for marriage. Then one festive night the betrothal would come to an end and the bridegroom, accompanied by his friends, would arrive with lights and songs and rejoicing and claim his bride and take her to his home. From that moment they were married.

When the angel appeared to me to announce my motherhood, I was still living at home. I was betrothed to Joseph but I had not yet gone to live with him.

After a few months I could not conceal my motherhood any longer. In the eyes of men everything had become plain, and very complicated.

I then understood the nature of faith in all its darkness and pain.

How could I explain myself to my mother?

How could I discuss things with Joseph?

It was a period of great distress and my only comfort came from telling myself over and over again that nothing is impossible with God, nothing is impossible with God.

It was for him to explain himself and I trusted him totally, but this did not take away my suffering which at times pierced my heart.

When could I find the words to tell people that the baby in my womb was the son of the Most High?

Meanwhile I didn't dare go out of the house, and once I saw a neighbour peering at me over the wall of the courtyard with obviously disapproving curiosity.

I was often very frightened and trembled at the thought of being denounced as an adulteress.

So little was needed for this to happen – Joseph only had to go to the synagogue to explain my situation and there would be no lack of fanatical people to follow him along armed with stones. It would not be the first time that an adulteress had been stoned to death in Nazareth.

But it is true: all is possible with God. And he explained himself.

He explained himself to Joseph, with the result that Joseph told me he had dreamed a dream and that he had not lost his trust in me but would marry me just the same.

Oh the joy I felt when he told me this! But what terror and darkness I had been through.

I came to understand that this is the very nature of faith and that we have to get used to living in darkness.

And something else happened which helped to alleviate my distress in those months.

You know that the angel had given me a sign to support me in my weakness. He told me that my cousin Elizabeth was in the sixth month of an amazing pregnancy – amazing, because all of us in the family knew her to be barren.

It was decided that I should go and visit her in Ain-Karim in Judea where she lived.

I didn't have to be persuaded to leave!

It was my mother's idea because she was worried about the

11

neighbours seeing me big with child, and she didn't want any gossip.

I left at night and I was really pleased to be getting away from Nazareth where there were so many inquisitive eyes and I couldn't tell everyone the facts of the situation.

I found my cousin already near her time, and very happy. She had longed for a child.

The Lord must have explained things to her too, because when I arrived she seemed to know everything, everything, everything.

She started to sing for joy, and I sang with her.

We must both have seemed mad, but mad with love.

And there was a third being who seemed to be mad with joy.

This was someone very small, the future John, who leapt in Elizabeth's womb as if to welcome Jesus who was in mine.

I shall never forget those days.

But Elizabeth, who knew all about faith, dark faith, and who had suffered so much in her life, said something to me which pleased me very much and seemed like a reward for all my loneliness in those months. She said:

'Blessed are you who believed' (Lk 1,44).*

And she repeated it every time she saw me and touched my belly, touched it as if to touch Jesus, the new Moses who was to come into the world.

The fire that had baked my bread was almost out. It was late at night and I was alone.

Mary's presence was now in my rosary. I held it in my hand and it invited me to pray.

I was cold and wrapped myself round in my *bournous*.†

Although it was now totally dark I had no desire to sleep.

I wanted to savour the meditation that Mary had granted me.

Above all I wanted to enter into the mystery of faith, true faith, painful faith, dark arid faith; I wanted to enter into it with strength and tenderness.

For it is not at all easy to believe, it is much easier to reason.

*RSV says 'Blessed is she who believed' – Elizabeth addressing Mary for a moment in the third person.

†An Arab cloak made of sheepskin.

12

It is not easy to accept a mystery that is too big for you and is always pushing back the frontiers of your weakness.

Poor Mary!

To have to believe that the baby in her womb was the son of the Most High. Yes, it was easy enough to conceive him in the flesh, considerably more demanding to conceive him in faith! A long haul indeed!

But the road had to be followed. There was no other choice.

Mary, when what you were asked to believe really frightened you, might you have turned back, decided it wasn't true, that it was pointless even to try to believe, that God couldn't possibly make himself man, that all this was a snare and a delusion — there was no messiah of salvation, chaos and irrationality ruled the world, death and not life would win at the finishing-post?

Never!

If belief is hard, non-belief is certain death.

If to hope against hope is heroic, despair is mortal anguish.

If to love costs you your blood, not to love is hell.

I believe, Lord!

I believe because I want to live.

I believe because I want to save my people from sinking.

I believe because the answer of belief is the only answer worthy of You who are transcendent, infinite, the creator, salvation, life, light, love, all in all.

What a strange, not to say a miraculous, thing: no sooner had I said the words 'I believe' with my whole heart than I saw the darkness of the night lifting.

I had to close my eyes because the night itself dazzled me with its peerless radiance.

Yes, nothing was brighter than that dark night, nothing more visible than the invisible God, nothing closer than the infinitely remote, nothing tinier than God's infinity.

Indeed God managed to fit into your little womb, Mary, and you kept him warm with your sweet body.

Mary!

My sister!

Blessed are you who believed — I say it to you tonight with rapture, as your cousin Elizabeth said it to you on that hot evening in Ain-Karim.

3

MY GOD, MY SON

During advent I found myself in the pale hot hills of
Béni-Abbès,* that fantastic oasis in the Sahara.

I wanted to prepare myself for Christmas in solitude, and
the place I had chosen was Ouarourout where water was
abundant and a small natural cave could serve as a chapel.

I set out after the feast of the Immaculate Conception (8
December) in wonderful weather and with a great longing to
be alone.

But the weather soon changed and the desert became cold
and grey due to the high mist that covered the sun.

And even my solitude was not what I expected for soon I
was discovered by Ali, son of Mohamed Assani. Ali was a
good friend who brought his eleven sheep to graze round
about and was thirsting for company and conversation. He
assured me that he couldn't find better or richer pastures for
his flock than near the well of Ouarourout.

He kept his distance, of course, because he knew that when I
was praying he had to keep away and not disturb me.

But the well was common property so naturally he took the
opportunity of coming near when I went to draw water, and
then he profited by the occasion to invite me to tea – having
taken all the necessaries from my tent.

Ali made tea very well and he loved drinking it with me; he
also liked my bread which I baked under the ashes.

Then off he went to the pastures and for the whole day
contented himself with keeping his eye on me from a distance
while he searched the sand for little fossils and archeological

*Charles de Foucauld, founder of the Little Brothers of Jesus, spent many years in
Béni-Abbès. (Tr.)

remains such as tips of arrows from the stone age which he could then come and sell to me.

The weather grew worse and I had to reinforce my tent ropes against the wind-storm which would surely follow. Wind-storms in the desert are appalling, developing as they do into sand-storms, and anyone who has been in the desert knows what a sand-storm is like.

To describe the sort of thing that can happen, suffice it to say that even at midday you have to switch on the headlights of the van if you want to see the track, and the windows and the paintwork are nearly worn away by the violence of the sand.

My one refuge was my cave, and, when the storm came, there I decided to stay night and day so as not to interrupt my retreat.

As for Ali, I had not seen him for a day or two so I told myself that he must have foreseen the storm and prudently returned to the fold and his father's tent situated about twelve kilometres from Ouarourout, at the intersection with the road to Bechar.

Not a bit of it!

There I was praying in my cave when he came rushing in, crook in hand and wild with worry.

'Come quickly, brother Carlo, come and help me. My sheep are lost, they're dying in the sand.'

I dashed to the van and together we plunged into the desert, a desert furious with blinding wind and sand.

It wasn't easy to find the sheep in that inferno. They were frightened and enfeebled and wandering helplessly in the gusts of sand and rain which had now started to fall.

I had never seen anything like it. Once again I realised how narrow is the line between life and death in the desert.

While I was at the steering wheel and trying not to get lost, Ali was pouncing on his sheep and piling them one by one into the van – they were weak with exhaustion and numb with fear.

Somehow we managed to get them into my cave, the only possible refuge from the breath-taking hurricane. So my little cave was full of wooliness, of bleating and of the acrid smell of sheep.

I was reminded of the cave at Bethlehem and I tried to get warm by snuggling up against the largest sheep – they were as drenched as I was and shivering in the evening dusk.

I took the eucharist from the tabernacle and hung the pyx round my neck under my cloak.

Naturally we did not manage to light the fire for supper, so we had to be satisfied with eating bread and a tin of sardines.

But Ali liked the sardines.

For myself, I wanted to pray, and I soon realised that things hadn't gone too badly for me in the turmoil of the storm.

Wasn't I living through a very special night?

It was near to Christmas.

I was in a cave with a shepherd.

I was cold.

There were sheep and the stench of dung.

Nothing was missing.

The eucharist that I had hung round my neck made me think of Jesus present there under the sign of bread, so like the sign of Bethlehem, the land of bread.

The night advanced. Outside the storm continued to rage over the desert.

Now all was silence in the cave.

The sheep filled up the available space.

Ali slept curled in his cloak with his head resting on the back of a sheep and with two lambs at his feet.

Meanwhile I prayed, reciting Luke's Gospel from memory:

'And while they were there, the time came for her to be delivered. And she gave birth to her first-born son and wrapped him in swaddling cloths, and laid him in a manger, because there was no place for them in the inn' (Lk 2,6). Then I was silent and waited.

Mary became my prayer and I felt her to be very very close to me.

Jesus was in the eucharist just there under my cloak.

All my faith, all my hope, all my love were united in one point.

I had no need to meditate, I only had to contemplate in silence. The whole night was at my disposal and dawn was still far off.

Was it a dream or was I awake?

I do not know and it is all the same.

For what is the difference between dream and reality when

the dream is about God coming into the world and the reality is a cave like the one described in the gospels?

To believe that God made himself man is the greatest possible dream for man. It would seem that such was his desire to unite earth and heaven that Christmas became the fulfilment of the desire.

So did I desire and dream Christmas, the coming of God into the world, or is it an amazing fact like a dream that has come true?

I think both, for the thing is so extraordinary; certainly the coming preceded the dream because none of us would have been capable of dreaming anything so unique and beautiful.

What is your opinion, Mary, for you are the person at the heart of the matter? Didn't it seem to you a dream to have a son like that?

It seemed to you real? To have conceived him in the flesh was nothing compared with the effort of conceiving him in faith.

To see a child, to see your own child, was easy, but to believe, to believe, while you were holding him up to pee in a corner, that he, your child, was the son of God, that was not easy at all.

Faith was certainly dark and painful for you, not only for us – your brothers and sisters – in the world of the living.

Under my cloak, hanging round my neck, I have the casket containing the eucharist. It is a small piece of bread consecrated through the faith of the Church. It is here with me, I love it, I adore it, but . . .

. . . it isn't easy to believe!

Isn't that what it's like, Mary?

Isn't it like that for you too?

There is no greater effort on earth than the effort to believe, to hope, to love: you know that.

Your cousin Elizabeth was right when she said, 'Blessed are you who believed!'

Yes, Mary, blessed are you who believed.

Blessed are you who help me to believe, blessed are you who were strong enough to accept the whole mystery of the nativity, and brave enough to lend your body to an event boundless in its greatness and equally boundless in its unbelievable littleness.

The incarnation was the meeting of extremes – the infinitely remote became infinitely close and the infinitely powerful became infinitely weak.

Mary, do you understand what you did?

You managed to stand firm beneath the weight of a boundless mystery.

You managed to stand firm before the radiance of the Eternal One when he was choosing your womb as a home where he could be warm.

You managed to stand firm when Satan leered at you and told you that God's transcendence could not possibly become incarnate in man's baseness.

How brave you were, Mary!

Only your humility could have helped you to withstand such an onslaught of alternate light and darkness.

All my life I have said: 'Our Father who art in heaven'. But let's face it, even this isn't so very easy.

To think that God the creator – infinite and omnipotent – should be not only a father but a loving father . . . this already presupposes a long progress in faith.

In the past it came more easily to think of a heavy-handed father, of a God who instilled fear, especially when there was thunder and lightning.

Not for nothing has the preoccupation with hell and eternal punishment haunted the nights of us sinners.

It is quite natural to be afraid of a creator-God, a God who is incommunicable, judgmental, unique.

Before such a powerful being as this we have no option but to sink down on our knees.

It is the uniqueness and transcendence of God that constitute the prime source of terror. When we read the Old Testament we are very aware of this and we notice the path that the people of God follow in their long exodus from slavery to the Promised Land. Here and there the voice of the prophet is already announcing love: 'Can a woman forget her sucking child, that she should have no compassion on the son of her womb? Even if these may forget, yet I will not forget you' (Is. 49,15).

But there is also the voice of the law-giver saying: 'The Lord . . . will by no means clear the guilty, visiting the iniquity of the fathers upon the children and the children's children, to the third and the fourth generation' (Exod. 34,7).

Read Leviticus, Numbers and especially Deuteronomy and you will see the truth of the phrase 'fear of God is the beginning of wisdom'.

But tonight I'm here and I'm not giving a thought to Leviticus or Deuteronomy.

I'm here in the stable beside Mary and I'm right inside the Gospel and the Gospel is saying: 'And she gave birth to her first-born' (Lk 2,7).

Transcendence has become incarnate, fear has become sweetness, I put my arms round incommunicability.

Distance has become closeness, God has become a son.

Do you understand the reversal that has taken place?

For the first time a woman could say with truth: 'My God, my son'.

So now I'm no longer frightened. If God is that baby lying on the straw in the cave, God cannot frighten me.

And if I can whisper 'my God, my son' sitting beside Mary, then paradise has come into my home and I am truly at peace.

I can be afraid of my father, yes, especially if I don't really know him; but of my son, never.

Of my son whom I hold in my arms, whom I cradle at my breast; of my son who asks me for protection and warmth, oh no.

I cannot be afraid.

I cannot be afraid.

I cannot be afraid any more. Peace, which is the absence of fear, now abides in me.

Now the only task that remains to me is to believe.

And believing is like generating. In faith I continue to generate Jesus as son.

This is what Mary did. It was easy enough for her to generate Jesus in the flesh: nine months were enough.

But to generate, give birth to, Jesus in faith – for that she needed her whole life from Bethlehem to Calvary.

Mary, like you I believe that this baby is both God and your son and I adore him.

I adore him in the casket I am wearing under my cloak

where he is hidden beneath the very frail sign of bread, frailer even then flesh.

I hear you, Mary, repeating every now and then, as at Bethlehem: 'My God, my son'.

And I answer you, 'My God, my son'.

It is this evening's rosary.

As it was then.

The animals' breathing warms the cave, as it did then.

4

'RACHEL WEEPING FOR HER CHILDREN' (Mt 2,18)

As God willed, the sand-storm abated and off Ali went to his pastures with his crook and his eleven sheep. I remained alone at Ouarourout to clean the dung out of the cave and to dry my bones out in the sun.

With the departure of the flock the imagery of Bethlehem went too, and I was left with the picture of Mary and Joseph trudging towards the south with the baby Jesus in their arms.

Why did they go so soon? Why did they set out on that rough road with such a tiny child in their care?

I read in Matthew: 'Behold an angel of the Lord appeared to Joseph in a dream and said, "Rise, take the child and his mother, and flee to Egypt, and remain there till I tell you, for Herod is about to search for the child, to destroy him." And he rose and took the child and his mother by night, and departed to Egypt' (Mt 2,13/14).

Jesus had hardly been born and already troubles were closing in on him. It seems unbelievable how difficult it is to live in our poor world!

And now Jesus is alone on the rough path, and tonight he may not find even a cave where he may shelter from the cold.

Matthew goes on: 'Then Herod, when he saw that he had been tricked by the wise men, was in a furious rage, and he sent and killed all the male children in Bethlehem and in all that region who were two years old or younger, according to the time which he had ascertained from the wise men.

'Then was fulfilled what was spoken by the prophet Jeremiah:

'A voice was heard in Ramah,
wailing and loud lamentation,
Rachel weeping for her children;

she refused to be consoled,
because they were no more' (Mt 2, 16/18).
It seems inconceivable that such atrocities should take place.
This is naked power and there are no limits to its abuse.
And it is the humble and the poor who pay for it.

So Herod, in his attempt to murder Jesus, organised one of
the many 'pogroms' of history.

I can imagine what happened that night! I can see the
soldiers surrounding the Bethlehem area and beginning their
carnage at nightfall. They would have a register of all the
newly-born babies, and there would be no difficulty in
smashing down the doors of the poor.

Oh the cry of those miserable mothers in the darkness!

Oh the horror of innocent blood!

Why?

Why?

Why?

And the whole enterprise to no purpose because Jesus had
escaped.

There was one broken link in the net and the little one had
flown like 'a bird from the snare of the fowlers' (Ps. 124).

Of course news like this could not be confined to one place.

The desert has its own telegraph system and news spreads at
the speed of wind.

A camel-driver also travelling south would have caught up
with the little party that included Jesus, and the words burning
within him would be quickly communicated.

Have you heard the news? Herod has had all the babies of
Bethlehem slaughtered. Not a single one escaped. It was
frightful. The soldiers came in the night and surrounded the
houses.

Mary listened in silence and drew her son to her breast
where her heart was beating so fast she thought it would
break.

Joseph watched her. I told you I was afraid; I told you I
didn't feel at ease in Bethlehem. I knew I had to flee, I knew it
in my bones. And then I had that dream . . .

The camel-driver spurred on his mount and went his way
leaving husband and wife speechless beside each other. Even
Jesus looked at the sun in silence.

My God, why?

INTRODUCTION TO THE PHOTOGRAPHS

If a believer meditates on the Gospel and prays in the context of the Word, he treads a path of faith which, through his personal experience of God, enables him to embody the events of Scripture within the taste, culture, art and liturgy of the period in which he lives.

It is from this that the many diverse expressions of thought and art flow – expressions which contribute to the advance of the people of God and bear witness to its depth and vitality over the centuries.

However it is sometimes beneficial to retrace the well-known path from the point of view of present-day reality, so as to nourish the power and beauty of God's message with new insights and get away from the weight of tradition.

So here follow several well-known pictures of the events recounted in the text; and also some modern photographs which, in my view, help to throw light on what happened in the past.

1. *The Annunciation (Simone Martini).*

2. *The Nativity (Giotto).*

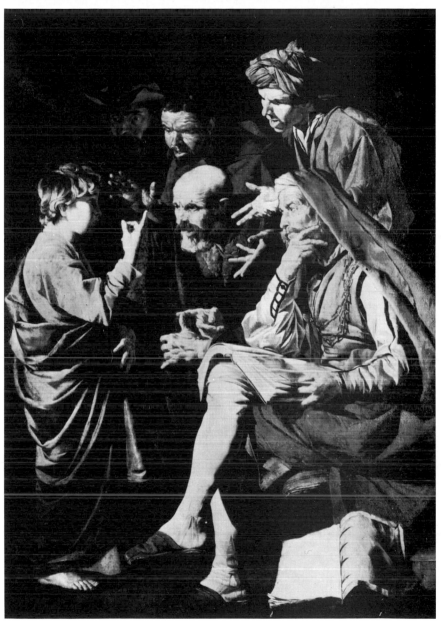

3. *Jesus among the doctors (Matthias Stromer).*

4.   *Mary's son is born in a humble cave.*

5. *Jesus in Joseph's arms (in the reconstruction of a 'living crib').*

6.   *The flight into Egypt, after the massacre of the innocents.*

7. *Mary settles down in Nazareth on her return from Egypt.*

My God, why?

My God, why?

What a night it was!

What a night!

What a night!

It's easy to think about God when all is going well, but to think about him in this darkness is hard indeed!

Mary, *you* say something to me.

But Mary said nothing.

She felt as if the tip of a sword was entering her heart.

She remembered the words spoken by the aged Simeon in the temple when she took Jesus there for the purification: 'Behold this child is set for the fall and rising of many in Israel, and for a sign that is spoken against (and a sword will pierce through your own soul also)' (Lk 2,35).

She could not get out of her mind all the babies she knew in Bethlehem, children of the same tribe of David, born at the same time as her son.

The sword pierced deep down into her mother's heart.

Why them and not Him?

Why did the Almighty allow the massacre?

Why didn't he protect them?

Why didn't he strike Herod dead?

Why?

Why?

But there was no answer.

Mary was bent double with grief on that parched track.

Joseph was as if drained in the depths of his being.

Jesus, wrapped in a little cloth, looked rapturously at the sun as it set in the dark red glow of the sky.

The ass nibbled a shrub by the side of the track.

Yes, it is not easy to believe in God, harder still to hope in his organising presence, superhuman to love men when they are murderers.

What should I do?

Tomorrow will see a new dawn and life continues.

How can I ever again join you in reciting your exalting prayer, the Magnificat, Mary, now that my eyes and yours are filled with the appalling spectacle of Herod's pogrom in Bethlehem?

And entirely on account of your son!

How can I possibly join you in saying 'My soul magnifies the Lord' or 'He has put down the mighty from their thrones, and exalted those of low degree'?

Because in fact you are bowed down with suffering and Herod is up there on his throne. Your heart is embittered and the poor are despised.

Power, not you, governs history.

And yet . . .

And yet it is not like that. Indeed we could say that it was ultimately Herod – power – who was made to look ridiculous.

Did he succeed in killing Jesus?

What did his cunning strategy – the encircling of Bethlehem at night with his soldiers – in fact achieve?

One broken link in the net and the trap did not work.

He had not done his homework.

What a snub to power!

So yes, it is true: 'He has scattered the proud in the imagination of their hearts' (Lk 1,51).

It is true. His plan was a flop.

But how about the others?

The sacrifice of so many innocent children?

Yet we can say of them that they fought the good fight, that they accomplished their mission.

This is the important point. By bringing the blows down on their own heads, the innocents prevented Christ from being killed in his flight; by calling the soldiers' attention to their own little bodies, they enabled the Messiah to escape the carnage; by employing the soldiers' time for as long as the massacre lasted, they brought salvation to Jesus.

It was essential that Jesus should not die that night. So they had to pay the price for him.

The hour of our death is not important. What is important is to fulfil our mission.

Jesus would fulfil his mission later on Calvary; the innocents fulfilled theirs during that night.

Those with power did not put the history of salvation off course, they merely attempted to, and they were 'scattered' (Lk 1,51).

Yes, Mary, say your Magnificat again tonight on this

parched track, and say it in full. Say it because tonight again you are involved in God's grand design and no-one can touch you if God does not wish it.

Say it!

Say it because no-one can touch your Jesus even though he is so small and defenceless.

Say it because history is in God's hands, not men's.

Say it because the Pharoahs have one by one been put down, and the poor have been freed.

Say it!

And I want to say it with you.

And while you are saying it I'm sure that the little martyrs will gather around you like angels, one by one, already transfigured in the Kingdom of light for which they fought, bearing witness with their death rather than with words to their Saviour's arrival.

How I would love to be one of them, Mary!

'My soul magnifies the Lord
and my spirit rejoices in God my Saviour,
for he has regarded the low estate of his handmaiden.
For behold, henceforth all generations will call me blessed;
for he who is mighty has done great things for me,
and holy is his name.
And his mercy is on those who fear him
from generation to generation.
He has shown strength with his arm,
he has scattered the proud in the imagination of their hearts,
he has put down the mighty from their thrones,
and exalted those of low degree;
he has filled the hungry with good things,
and the rich he has sent empty away.
He has helped his servant Israel,
in remembrance of his mercy,
as he spoke to our fathers,
to Abraham and to his posterity for ever.'

It is still a long long way to Egypt.
Courage, Joseph, let's go on.
God provides.

5

NAZARETH

Egypt was our place of refuge for several years.

It really is a place where people can hide, with all those reeds along the Nile and those bays and inlets that kept little Moses safe.

We were kept safe too even though we were foreign, poor and defenceless.

Every day God provided for us in our weakness.

Of course we suffered at being so far from home, so alone, but it had to be like that for God's plan to be accomplished.

For in fact God called his son, the new Moses, out of the land of Egypt: 'and out of Egypt I called my son' (Hos. 11,1).

When the time came we set out towards the north.

By now Jesus had grown sturdier and stronger. And Herod was dead.

The journey was long but not too difficult.

Jesus made us very happy; we noticed that he often looked over towards Jerusalem with special interest.

But Joseph decided that it would be unwise to settle too close to Jerusalem, even though Herod was dead. It was impossible to forget what had happened a few years before.

Jerusalem is one of the most treacherous of capital cities. For one thing there are two powers there – the political and the religious.

The situation was not exactly clear, and we preferred to keep our distance.

We settled in Nazareth in Galilee where there was greater freedom and where I, Mary, had lived as a girl.

Joseph would have preferred Bethlehem, the land of his tribe, but he had no difficulty in establishing himself in Nazareth, especially as he was a skilled artisan.

He set up shop and we embarked on a happy period of our lives.

Jesus grew and became strong, filled with wisdom; and the favour of God was upon him (Lk 2,40).

He was a lovely boy and he helped Joseph in the workshop.

I watched him as one watches a mystery.

I could never look on him simply as my son.

I simply could not manage it, and naturally this made me suffer.

Gradually I realised that this was my mission, that there was no other way, but I suffered.

The mystery of his birth constantly overwhelmed me; the thought that Jesus was the son of God forced me to get out of myself and enter the realm of faith.

This was always painful.

It was as if I had never been able to grasp the secret of my son in its deepest significance.

I had conceived him in my flesh once and for all, but as to conceiving him in faith, this was a continuous process, without pause, right to the end.

Then there occurred an episode that made a great impression on me; I thought about it frequently in an effort to understand what was going on.

Every year we went on a pilgrimage to Jerusalem for the feast of the Passover, and as Jesus was twelve we naturally took him with us.

What bustle and confusion that pilgrimage was! Yet what joy, what life it enshrined!

Spring seemed to invade everything, the children ran wild.

In Jerusalem an event took place that brought something totally new into my relationship with Jesus.

As we were setting out on our return journey 'the boy Jesus stayed behind in Jerusalem. His parents did not know it, but supposing him to be in the company they went a day's journey, and they sought him among their kinsfolk and acquaintances' but did not find him (Lk 2,43/44).

This was not a pleasant surprise. For the first time we had lost contact with him.

We returned at once to Jerusalem to look for him, in a state of anxiety bordering on panic.

What on earth could have happened?

I had no doubt at all that he had chosen to escape from us.

And yet I was incapable of making the link, and Joseph was as anxious as I was.

It was as if the mystery of him and his being had suddenly deepened, and as if he had found it necessary to distance himself from us.

I felt the sword prophesied by Simeon entering my heart.

We pursued an anguished search for him like any other father or mother, but I realised that something else was at work.

It was out of the question that Jesus was behaving just like any other boy. If he was behaving like this it was in order to tell us something new. His escape had to do with an advance in faith that we were making together.

The time had come when we had to realise that our motherhood and fatherhood were altogether relative to his freedom.

Jesus was becoming aware of being 'the son of God' (Mt 4,3) rather than the son of Mary and Joseph.

Indeed when we finally found him in the temple he said plainly enough: 'Did you not know that I must be in my Father's house?' (Lk 2,49).

This was the truth, but the truth had the power to plunge the sword deeper into my heart.

My suffering derived from his isolating of himself, from my seeing that he was making a space for himself that I could not invade, and this was very painful to my nature as a mother.

I had to give him his freedom, but this cost me a lot.

Yet I did not suspect that this absence of three days foreshadowed the terrible three days' absence that was to occur at the time of his death.

He wanted to free himself from *me* so as to be free for *everyone*.

He wanted to free himself from *me* so as to die for *all*.

Returning to Nazareth and to our everyday life, I realised that many things had changed and that, as far as I was concerned, a new period had begun.

Faith was becoming more purified and Jesus's transparency was increasing.

My temptation to be a possessive mother had received a

tremendous blow. 'Did you not know that I must be in my Father's house?'

I could not get this constant refrain out of my mind. No, I didn't know, and that's why I didn't understand.

Indeed Luke's Gospel says explicitly about Joseph and myself: 'And they did not understand the saying which he spoke to them' (Lk 2,50).

It isn't easy to understand the infinite transparency to which God calls us in our deepest feelings.

It is a pilgrimage, and a pilgrimage exists for us to learn, and on the way we often get tired and would like to stop and rest.

I, as a young mother, wanted to think that my son was mine, mine alone. . .

Whereas I had to face the fact that my son belonged to everyone, yes, to everyone!

As I returned to Nazareth after the pilgrimage, on that memorable return journey, I could not get out of my mind what happened to Abraham on Mount Moriah – when he was asked by God to sacrifice his son Isaac.

It is not easy to sacrifice a son, especially when he is the only one, as Jesus was for me.

Another thing that the period in Nazareth taught me, the period spent in Jesus's school, was the divinity of communal things.

If God was with me, in my house, among my things, then everything was divine. Heaven and earth were fused without any interruption in continuity.

So where lay the entry into the Kingdom if Jesus was already with me?

I was already in the Kingdom. What mattered was to become aware of it.

Indeed he often said, 'The Kingdom of God is in the midst of you' (Lk 17,21).

This is very important, because it gives the things of the earth their proper value.

We on earth are often tempted to look on work, bread, jobs, as secular areas of activity, devoid of God, or anyway neutral where he is concerned.

But it isn't like that. If Jesus is present in our work, then our work is sacred. If God lives in our job, then our job is prayer. If

Jesus is in our house, then our house is a church.

Yes, this is one of the most important things that we should understand: the frontier of the invisible lies in faith, not in reality.

After the incarnation reality became divinised because Jesus entered reality; thus by touching reality we touch the divine.

If the Word was made flesh, all flesh was made the Word.

The whole universe became God's Word.

The universe's visible side is the sign of the Word, its invisible side is the sign of the Spirit.

No, men will not flee from the infinite claims of reality, informed by God as it henceforth is, and inhabited by him.

It is not possible.

You can now understand the importance of faith and hope and charity, all of which carry you beyond the frontier of the visible.

In faith you talk with God, in hope you listen to God, in charity you experience God.

Have you understood?

Reality is the context of God.

Nazareth for me was the context of God because it was my reality.

And I didn't have to be possessive about it.

It is one of the most insidious of temptations – being possessive about something.

By being possessive about things you take away their transparency, their freedom, their identity.

By being possessive about creation you become its slave.

Each thing has its own vocation, and freedom is the voice of vocation.

I had my son Jesus, but my son Jesus was perfectly free and our love developed within reciprocal freedom.

How difficult it is to live the life of love without falling into possessiveness – which is slavery.

And we are called to freedom. For us Nazareth was the school of freedom and Jesus was freedom.

It was this that taught us and kept us going: freedom from money, freedom from idols, freedom from public opinion, freedom from fear, freedom from everything.

We had to possess as if we did not possess, mourn as though

we were not mourning, rejoice as if we were not rejoicing (cf. 1 Cor. 7,30). In our little home we felt that 'all are yours; and you are Christ's; and Christ is God's' (1 Cor. 3,23).

And meanwhile things went on and he helped me with his presence and love.

Mutual love formed the basis of our relationship.

However he always overtook me and I felt smaller than he as he grew bigger.

I was always amazed by his silence and had to nourish my hope just with waiting.

I never quite understood when he was going to start on his real mission, and every day was good for increasing my longing.

When he recited passages of scripture from memory I trembled and was uplifted at the same time.

He very much loved Isaiah; I would say that his favourite passage was the one about the Lord's servant.

I think he grew to identify himself with this passage; I would go so far as to say that he gradually became aware that he was the Lord's servant.

He then developed a sweetness all his own, and he murmured phrases which I later recognised when he was teaching the beatitudes.

Blessed are the poor in spirit.

Blessed are those who mourn.

Blessed are those who are persecuted.

Nazareth was certainly the best time of my life as a mother and the best time of my life with him.

It fell to me to be beside him when he was little, and I was so happy; now it fell to me to be beside him when he was grown up.

All I wanted was to be always beside him.

I knew nothing; he himself became my wisdom.

I felt I didn't even need to go to the synagogue because his word was enough for me.

When I think about that time I feel exalted.

I seem to have been always praying – better than being always at prayer.

In any case, what is prayer if not 'being with God' and I was with God twenty-four hours out of twenty-four.

So was he, as could be seen.

You only had to look at him. There was perfect unity between his thoughts and his actions.

He was always in harmony with himself and yet he obeyed a reality that dwelt deep within him.

Yes, he was dwelt in.

'Thou art in me, and I in thee' he often whispered, therefore 'we are one' (cf. Jn 17,21/23).

And I knew he was speaking of the Father.

6

DO WHATEVER HE TELLS YOU

When we asked him if his hour had come he did not reply. It seemed as if even he had no choice but to wait.

I heard him often repeat that phrase which occurs in Mark 13,32: of that day and that hour 'no one knows, not even the angels in heaven, nor the Son, but only the Father'.

He lived in a state of expectation, like the rest of us. He arrogated nothing to himself; everything depended on the Father.

He was the only thing that mattered: the Father.

Nevertheless we sensed that things were coming to a head.

Quite early he had made friends in Capernaum where he went from time to time. He felt rather isolated in Nazareth and I was well aware that when his wings spread he would choose Capernaum as his landing-place.

One day he told me that he would like me to meet these friends of his. He waited for a suitable opportunity and this came of its own accord.

There was to be a marriage at Cana in Galilee to which I was invited and so was he.

It seemed an excellent opportunity for a first meeting.

He stopped off at Capernaum and collected his friends.

Cana was along the same road and there we met for the marriage.

I was amazed at the number of people Jesus brought with him. Enough to make quite heavy inroads into the cellar.

The best was made of a bad job: it seemed to me that a following of that size was a bit much considering the smallness of the family from whom the invitation had come.

There was a lot of noise and it was difficult to make out what sort of talk was going on.

The business of the marriage was just an excuse – because Jesus's companions were all engrossed in conversation about the Messiah and the Kingdom.

There was a general atmosphere of exaltation, and the wine served to foster and add to the excitement.

It looked as if they were planning to lay siege to the temple; the eyes of those nearest to Jesus were shining like stars.

Jesus was obviously the leader.

Naturally with all those guests celebrating the first thing that was going to run out was the wine.

I soon noticed that the bride and bridegroom were getting worried. Though they continued to smile they looked with definite anxiety at the steward of the feast who was a relation of ours.

There was no question about it, the wine had run out. For the first time in my life I felt invaded by the same exaltation as the disciples. Heaven and earth were facing each other in that little courtyard at Cana where our friends' marriage was taking place.

No, the wine would not run out, for the very good reason that among us was someone who would give us the wine of the Kingdom.

Everything was possible with him.

Shouting, singing, merry-making were raising the roof.

I approached Jesus with a beating heart and took hold of his arm. I said: 'They have no wine' (Jn 2,3).

He looked at me rather sternly, yet I seemed to note in him a moment of hesitation.

But I was feeling so exalted that I paid no attention either to his look or to the rather harsh words he said to me. I wanted to force his hand.

I was so aroused that I was absolutely confident of what I was saying. My head was on fire.

I said to the servants with utter conviction: 'Do whatever he tells you' (Jn 2,5).

Then I tried to hide myself in the crowd so that no-one could see me, and I began to pray with all my strength:

'Everything is possible with God,
Everything is possible with God,
Everything is possible with God.'

This phrase had always obsessed me ever since the angel of

the Lord had told me about the coming of Jesus.

Yes, everything is possible with God.

That day was a memorable one, and everyone was filled with joy.

That wine seemed to go to everybody's head.

Yes, everything was possible with God, and the river of wine was a symbol of the joy bestowed by the encounter with God and the bliss of his embrace.

We sang, we danced. Our friends' marriage had become the symbol of another marriage, much more radical and joyful: the marriage between man and God.

Yes, John was right when he placed the marriage at Cana as the first joyful encounter between the Church and Jesus.

It was a feast because the encounter with God is a feast.

Later, at Pentecost, we were to experience another kind of exaltation, but in that little courtyard at Cana beneath the slopes of Tabor we were already happy because God was with us.

Israel's loneliness was over.

Israel's widowhood had been forgotten.

Peter and John and James were at Cana.

So were Andrew (Simon Peter's brother), Philip of Bethsaida, Nathaniel (who spoke badly of Nazareth but was enraptured by every word that Jesus uttered) and many others.

After the event of the wine I did not dare show myself any more.

Although I was very happy about what had happened, I felt I had pushed myself forward and that now I ought to take a back place.

I certainly did not want to embarrass Jesus with my presence, so I promised myself that I would henceforth live in concealment and always keep silent.

It was the twelve who mattered now, and some of them made a point of pushing themselves forward to attract Jesus's attention.

It was obviously no easy task to keep such a heterogeneous group together, and although on that day they all gave the impression that they 'believed in him' (Jn 2,11), dark and painful days would not be lacking.

Above all it would be difficult to convince everyone that Jesus and Jesus alone could provide the wine that they had been drinking.

I understood with joy that the true mystery of the Church and of the apostolate lay precisely in this fact, and I saw what difficulty men would have in accepting this mystery.

Peter was already beginning to feel that he was the leader of the group and had a special importance, but even he could not have done what Jesus did.

Jesus was unique because he was God.

Only he could pour the wine of the Kingdom into everyone's cup.

Oh yes, the rest of us, the servants, everyone, could prepare the jars, fill them with water, wait to see what happened, even do the pouring out.

But the mystery of that wine was God himself.

On that day I already realised that there would always be a temptation for us in the Church to arrogate to ourselves the possibility of providing that wine, without waiting for Jesus to do so.

But it would be a wine totally without conviction.

Men can provide wine from their vineyards, but not the wine of the Kingdom.

It was necessary for the Church to be contemplative, but if she had forgotten that crucial act of waiting for everything to come from God (for instance, the transformation of that wine) she would have become a huge shop that could sell many things, but certainly nothing divine.

So I resolved always to try to remind people to act as if everything depended on ourselves, but to wait in prayer as if everything depended upon God, because the Kingdom is God's, not ours, even if – as it seems – we help in bringing it to fruition.

I learnt something else that day in Cana – joy.

If you drink the wine offered you by God himself then you are full of joy.

Oh no, it does not follow that this joy is always easy, free from pain and tears, but it is joy.

You may perhaps drink the wine that is the fruit of God's will when you are bowed down with sorrow and adversity, and yet you experience joy.

God is joy even if you are crucified.

God is joy even if you die.

God is always joy.

God is joy because he knows how to transform the water of our poverty into the wine of resurrection.

Nothing can resist this transforming power, his infinite capacity for renewing things, his perennial making-new of the new heaven and the new earth.

Sufficient for us to believe and to hope and to love, and the miracle always takes place.

And joy is our grateful response.

Yes, a disciple of Jesus

should live in joy

should spread joy

should be drunk with joy.

And this will always be his true apostolate.

And another thing I learnt from the wine that Jesus bestowed with such liberality: the total equality of the People of God.

The wine of the Kingdom was drunk by everyone without distinction, the whole company made merry, it was a free gift to one and all.

The last could draw on it as much as the first, divine reality was for all, prophecy was for all, holiness was for all, priesthood was for all.

Now I understood what Jesus meant when he told me about the Kingdom and about how all redeemed men would be 'a chosen race, a royal priesthood, a holy nation, God's own people' (1 Pet. 2,9).

The various castes with their shameful ostentation were a thing of the past, exclusiveness was finished, the poor drank at the same table as the rich.

The Church intoxicated with that wine was a universal Church: there was no longer 'Jew nor Greek . . . male nor female' (Gal. 3,28).

They could all prophesy as soon as the spirit of that wine possessed them.

They could all be holy because he who had quenched their thirst was holy.

They could all be priests because that wine was distributed by the eternal priest.

On that day I, Mary of Nazareth, felt myself to be a priest of the Most High and called on to offer my Jesus as the eternal sacrifice.

7

LIFE AND PAIN

No sooner had Jesus set out on his public life than he encountered opposition; no sooner had he started to distribute life than he began to suffer.

The two things were connected. It is not possible to dispense life without drinking the cup of pain. It always hurts to give birth.

Official circles were resolutely opposed to Jesus from the outset; they were too far removed from him; their thoughts were not his thoughts.

But they let things ride because they were so sure of themselves and looked on Jesus as being like any other provincial prophet – they had all had brief careers.

In any case Jesus had a special liking for subjects that were not very interesting to senior officials – for instance, sinners. He made it very plain that he had come for *them*, that he felt solidarity with *them*, and close to *them*.

Indeed he lost no time in going down to the river Jordan, to John the Baptist, because he wanted John to baptise him, for all the world as if he was a public sinner – he, Jesus, the Holy of Holies.

John did not wish to do it so put up some resistance, but Jesus insisted.

Jesus began from the bottom, the bottom that was made up of real poverty and unremitting defeat.

Sinners felt his closeness to them and quickly became his friends.

Jesus was less severe than John and never spoke of axes laid to the root of trees. He never frightened the little ones.

As he carried the label of friend to prostitutes and publicans, troubles could hardly fail to arise, and precisely in the area of religion.

Indeed . . .

The first to become aware of the situation were the Pharisees who themselves wore the badge of purity, truth and spirituality.

The Pharisees never lost an opportunity for attacking him on his own ground.

Written into their law was the perfection of Israel and they could not tolerate Jesus's attitude of compassion and forebearance: they saw it as weakness.

But Jesus was not to be deflected and he was more and more surrounded by the poor. In his preaching he shifted the emphasis from law to love, from punishment to mercy, from harshness to compassion.

The fact that men were sinners more or less everyone was agreed on. The novelty in Jesus was that sinners could be loved.

Yes, it was quite a departure for Israel, accustomed as it was to cursing the sinner and desiring his eradication from the holy city.

Whereas it seemed that Jesus not only retained a regard for the sinner, but clearly loved him, and loved him with a special love.

The situation gave scandal because it was Israel's practice to extol the men of law and the perfectionists of the Torah.

To place trust in an adulteress and confidence in a publican was going completely against the tide.

The conversion of the publican, Zaccheus, was unforgettable. He was a rich man who had been involved in illicit dealings and been cast out by the custodians of morality – so for him, a public sinner, to see himself favoured by Jesus and worthy to sit at table with the Holy One . . . well, he just couldn't contain himself!

What wouldn't he have done for Jesus who went on saying: 'For the Son of man came to seek and to save the lost' (Lk 19,10).

Yes, whoever felt lost clung to Jesus.

Watching the crowds that followed him you had the impression that only sinners understood him. Better still: only those who knew they were sinners understood him.

These people had been able to recognise through their sinfulness the true eternal poverty of man.

They were the real poor and needed Jesus in order to be saved.

Israel's frontier was no longer a piece of land to be conquered but holiness to be lived.

Israel's enemies were no longer the Canaans or the Philistines but its own pride, its sensuality, its selfishness, its fear.

The whole of Exodus had become simply the sign of another exodus, a truly universal one encompassing all men born of women, an exodus having as its Promised Land the freedom that God was telling them about, the freedom of the sons of the Most High.

It was in Jerusalem that Jesus underwent his real ordeals.

Though this was the city that concerned him most, he distrusted it most.

In Galilee he felt at home and so long as he was surrounded by the poor he felt at ease.

But when he walked in the streets of Jerusalem and saw the faces of the powerful and the spies of the great peeping over the low walls, then he suffered.

Nothing else was a problem: Jerusalem was the problem.

That was where the clash would come; it was plain to all and if we had had our way he would never have gone back to Jerusalem.

But he . . .

It was necessary . . . And back he went.

He went back.

One day I had the distinct feeling that the question was really political and that the rest was just outward appearance.

The people surrounding Jesus wanted power.

They did not want to accept defeat.

In last analysis they were expecting a conquering Messiah: they were irritated by his preaching about the beatitudes and non-violence.

Adherents of similar messianic visions were in the majority.

Jesus would not have been able to explain himself: they would have overthrown him.

It is sad but true: Israel was incapable of recognising the face of its Messiah, of its Christ, the face of the suffering Servant.

It wanted another one.

Jesus was unsatisfactory; a conqueror was required.

The political situation of servitude to the Romans justified the desire for liberation.

If Moses had done what he did and put liberation into people's minds, then the new Moses should do as much and fight against the Romans.

Jesus was silent on political issues, he tried not to betray himself, but he made it very plain to his disciples that henceforth freedom lay in men's hearts.

The great Exodus accomplished by Moses to get free from the Pharoahs was only the image of a permanent exodus, the exodus from ourselves, from our servitudes, from the Pharoah hidden within each one of us.

Jesus was henceforth the Moses of every man on earth, the authentic liberator of the spirit; to return to political issues was to return to the eternal ghetto.

The salvation proposed by Jesus was universal: freedom from death.

Israel did not want to accept a project of this kind and totally failed to recognise Christ's face.

What suffering for Jesus and for me!

I say for me, Mary, because even among the apostles there was no desire to support Jesus's design concerning the beatitudes.

Even among us there were zealots who believed in weapons, in power and in the triumphant Christ.

Right up to the end.

People were very very far from understanding Jesus's revelation concerning reality, life and God.

Especially God.

They still had a mental picture of God as someone who ruled with a rod of iron, jealous of his prerogatives and desirous to see a world as regulated and untroubled as an old-fashioned convent.

Morality was their chief concern and their zeal found expression in the perfection of the law and the punishment of sinners.

It would seem that there was only one joy remaining to a God rejected by disobedient and sinful men – that of building a hell to punish them.

Small-minded men forged for themselves a small-minded

God incapable of innovation and salvation.

How remote was Jesus's way of thinking from the moralistic preoccupations of the Temple!

And how circumscribed was man's vision concerning the true things of God!

And God was in the act of revealing his identity in Jesus . . .

Heaven was exploding on earth!

So bright was the light that it made everyone blind.

Even Satan was taken in by the brilliance of the flash and never recovered from his astonishment.

And what was the revelation?

It was the revelation of a poor and suffering and defeated God.

Man who had got used to the idea of thunder and punishment falling from heaven found himself faced with Jesus dead on the cross.

Many faces of the Messiah had been dreamed up by men at prayer, but the best guess was obviously Isaiah's: the face of the suffering Servant.

God was love clothed in poverty and pain so as to save man who had fallen into poverty and pain.

God was love identifying himself with the loved one, man; and sinking right down to the depths of man's sin so as to save him.

Death was for Jesus the supreme moment of his supreme poverty.

God had chosen the path of poverty to save man, and no moment of his journey was so steeped in poverty as the moment of his death.

A dead God was absolute poverty: it was impossible to go further than that.

By reaching the depths of this dark abyss, Christ had reached all the people whom the Father had chosen to be his sons but who had forfeited this sonship through disobedience.

By entering into the chaos produced by the perversity of a confused and deluded mankind, Jesus had identified himself with what was lost through showing that there was salvation even for sin.

By taking hardness-of-heart into its embrace, the power of love had been able to melt it. The prodigal son's flight had

51

become a positive act because it brought to light the depths of the father's mercy.

Love had won, man was saved.

Freedom had inherited the earth.

To accept death as an act of love is not easy, and I believe that this was the climax of Christ's achievement in his travail towards love.

And it is for us to imitate him, even in our weakness.

But death, real death, is not physical death; this is only the outward sign of it, the horrible visible palpable representation of it.

Real death is separation from God, and this is unbearable; real death is faithlessness, hopelessness, lovelessness.

We all know what pain and sadness are, for we have all experienced them and are all immersed in them.

Real death is the chaos where man finds himself when he disobeys the Father, it is the tangled web to which he is reduced by his passions, it is the total defeat of all his dreams of greatness, it is the disintegration of his whole personality.

Real death is emptiness, darkness, desolation, despair, hatred, destruction.

So . . . Christ agreed to enter into this death, into this separation, so as to identify himself with all who were in separation, and to save them.

When he had touched the depths of their despair he announced hope with his resurrection.

When he was immersed in their darkness he made the brightness of truth burst forth with his resurrection.

When engulfed in the abyss of their lovelessness he showed them the infinite joy of love with his resurrection.

By rising from the dead Christ made all things new.

By rising from the dead he opened new heavens.

By rising from the dead he opened new life.

Anyone who dreams of a triumphant Church in this world is mistaken and is reverting to the past without knowing it, or rather he is reverting to his childish conception of God and man.

The true Church is the Church of the defeated, of the weak, of the poor, of those on the fringe of society.

It is a pity that the great gatherings of Christians too often take place in St Peter's Square where Bernini, son of a pagan period sick with triumphalism, designed everything as a triumph.

We must beware!

In St Peter's Square there are many lusty people to shout hosannahs!

I know something about that!

But we must beware!

In that square there is no sign of the Church's agony, of men's agony . . . and everything can go wrong if I forget the reality, even when everything seems on the surface to be fine.

Rallies of Christians are more suitable in hospitals, in prisons, in shanty towns, in mental homes, where people cry, where people suffer, where the devastation of sin is being physically endured, sin in the form of the arrogance of the rich and the powerful.

Jesus's face is there and reveals itself there because it is there that 'the lost' are to be sought and saved (Lk 19,10).

Hand-clapping is a drug and Christians should be on their guard against it.

Huge processions should be postponed until later on in the Kingdom.

The rich materials and brocades of the liturgy should be used for covering the naked of the Third World, and the wealth of the Church sent to feed children dying of hunger.

The Gospel is much more explicit about man's real triumph and the way to pray and express holiness.

Mary at the foot of the cross made me see what Jesus's face was like.

It was the face of man transfigured by crucified love.

No other face could have been more beautiful.

8

HE IS RISEN

On the day after the sabbath, Mary Magdalene came to the tomb early, while it was still dark, and saw that the stone had been taken away from the tomb.

So she ran, and went to Simon Peter and the other disciple, the one whom Jesus loved, and said to them: 'They have taken the Lord out of the tomb, and we do not know where they have laid him'.

Peter then came out with the other disciple, and they went toward the tomb. They both ran, but the other disciple outran Peter and reached the tomb first.

And stooping to look in, he saw linen cloths lying there, but he did not go in.

Then Simon Peter came, following him, and went into the tomb and saw the linen cloths lying, and the napkin which had been on his head, not lying with the linen cloths but rolled up in a place by itself.

Then the other disciple, who reached the tomb first, also went in, and he saw and believed.

For as yet they did not know the scripture, that he must 'rise from the dead'.

But Mary stood weeping outside the tomb.

And as she wept she stooped to look into the tomb, and she saw two angels in white, sitting where the body of Jesus had lain, one at the head and one at the feet.

They said to her, 'Woman, why are you weeping?' She said to them, 'Because they have taken away my Lord, and I do not know where they have laid him'.

Saying this, she turned round and saw Jesus standing, but she did not know that it was Jesus. Jesus said to her, 'Woman, why are you weeping? Whom do you seek?'

Supposing him to be the gardener, she said to him, 'Sir, if you have carried him away, tell me where you have laid him, and I will take him away'.

Jesus said to her, 'Mary'. She turned and said to him in Hebrew, 'Rabboni!' (which means Teacher).

Jesus said to her, 'Do not hold me, for I have not yet ascended to the Father; but go to my brethren and say to them, I am ascending to my Father and your Father, to my God and your God'.

Mary Magdalene went and said to the disciples, 'I have seen the Lord'; and she told them that he had said these things to her (cf. Jn 20, 1/18).

On the evening of that day, the first day of the week, the doors being shut where the disciples were, for fear of the Jews, Jesus came and stood among them and said to them, 'Peace be with you'. When he had said this he showed them his hands and his side. Then the disciples were glad when they saw the Lord.

Jesus said to them again, 'Peace be with you. As the Father has sent me, even so I send you'. And when he had said this he breathed on them and said to them, 'Receive the Holy Spirit. If you forgive the sins of any, they are forgiven; if you retain the sins of any, they are retained.'

Now Thomas, one of the twelve, called the Twin, was not with them when Jesus came. So the other disciples told him, 'We have seen the Lord'.

But he said to them, 'Unless I see in his hands the print of the nails, and place my finger in the mark of the nails, and place my hand in his side, I will not believe'.

Eight days later his disciples were again in the house, and Thomas was with them. The doors were shut, but Jesus came and stood among them and said, 'Peace be with you'. Then he said to Thomas, 'Put your finger here and see my hands; and put your hand and place it in my side; do not be faithless, but believing'.

Thomas answered him, 'My Lord and my God!' Jesus said to him, 'Have you believed because you have seen me? Blessed are those who have not seen and yet believe' (cf. Jn 20,19/29).

Mary, the reason why I wanted to quote the whole of John's chapter about the resurrection is because I did not quite know how to talk about it myself.

What do you say about it?

Is this account of an event of this kind sufficient for people enclosed in their darkness?

And before anything: What did you yourself feel when Mary Magdalene told you she had seen Jesus in the garden?

And when Peter and John came running to tell you they had found the tomb empty?

What happened on that day?

What does it mean to believe that Christ rose from the dead?

And did *you* see him during those days?

Why doesn't the Gospel talk about *you*?

You were the person most concerned.

You were his mother!

Why didn't he appear to *you*?

I have thought so much about the Gospel's silence on these matters!

Was Jesus alluding to you when he said to Thomas: 'Blessed are those who have not seen and yet believe' (Jn 20,29)?

Perhaps you were the only one who did not need to see in order to believe . . .

For you were blessed.

I think this was it.

And this is why you are our teacher in faith, and why Elizabeth's praise right at the beginning was the greatest praise that could be given you:

'Blessed are you who believed.'

You did not need to see in order to believe.

You believed in your risen son, and that was enough for you.

To believe in Jesus's resurrection means to believe without seeing.

And I want to believe without seeing, like you.

I don't want to feel the need to see: better, I don't even ask to see any more.

When in front of the tabernacle I often say: 'Jesus, I believe in your presence in the eucharistic bread'.

Then I say to myself: 'What would happen if the tabernacle opened and Jesus revealed his presence to me in some other form? If, for instance, he appeared to me under the sign of the man Jesus as I imagine him to myself when I think of him?'

This is what would happen. I would turn away and say to

him, 'No, I don't need another sign, the sign of bread is enough for me'.

Another sign would disturb me.

No, I do not want it.

It might be a trick of my senses.

Whereas in faith I feel safe and I say to you, in the Spirit, which is your Spirit, 'I believe in your resurrection from the dead. I believe in your presence in the eucharist'.

No, brothers and sisters, there is no point in seeking elsewhere: you will not find.

The only thing that matters is faith.

Other mental states will let you down, sentimentality and fantasy will make you fanatical, visions will leave you unconvinced, research into the paranormal will alienate you from reality, weeping madonnas . . . they will not help you, indeed all short-cuts lead to superstition.

The only thing that remains is faith.

And it is through faith that I believe in Christ's resurrection.

And when I believe, I am invincible. 'This is the victory that overcomes the world: our faith' (1 Jn 5,4).

You tell me, Mary. What happened that morning? Was it easy for the infant Church, for Peter, for the apostles, for the disciples, to convince themselves that Christ had risen?

And what did their conviction come from?

From having seen?

And why didn't they believe the women who had seen (cf. Lk 24,11)?

From having seen?

And what had Mary Magdalene seen if even she thought Jesus was the gardener (cf. Jn 20,15)?

From having seen?

How is seeing possible when you can spend half the day with him on the road to Emmaus and not recognise him (cf. Lk 24,16)?

No, it is not with our eyes that we see Christ's resurrection: we see it in faith. Eyes are too deceptive, even if they see the sign.

Will it be easier with the word? Yes, certainly.

Especially when the word is the Word of God: 'And

beginning with Moses and all the prophets he interpreted to them in all the scriptures the things concerning himself' (Lk 24,27).

But even in the context of the word, faith is required because it is in faith that God reveals his presence.

'He took the bread and blessed, and broke it, and gave it to them. And their eyes were opened and they recognised him; and he vanished out of their sight' (Lk 24,30/31).

It is in faith that we encounter God.
It is in hope that we find his living embrace.
It is in charity that we experience God.
And faith is dark.
And hope is painful.
And charity is crucified.

Mary, help me to believe.
Tell me what it means to believe in the resurrection of your son.
Listen, I am telling you, and remember what I say.
When you see a forest ravaged by storms,
and earthquakes blasting the land
and fire burning down your home
say to yourself: I believe
that the forest will come to life again
the land will be calm again
and I shall remake my home.

When you hear rumours of war and people everywhere are dying of terror, when 'nation shall rise against nation and kingdom against kingdom' (Mt 24,7), say bravely to yourself, 'Jesus warned me of this and he added: "Look up and raise your heads, because your redemption is drawing near" ' (Lk 21,28).

When sin has you in its grip and you feel utterly defeated, say to yourself, 'Christ is risen from the dead and I shall rise from my sin'.

When old age or illness embitters your life, say 'Christ is risen from the dead and has made a new heaven and a new earth'.

When you see your son running away from home in search of adventure and your cherished dream as father or mother crumbles around you, say 'My son will not run away from God; he will come back because God loves him'.

When charity seems to have vanished for ever and you see men sunk in sin and drunk with treachery, say to yourself, 'They will touch the depths but they will return because no-one can live away from God'.

When the world seems a defeat for God and you are sick with the disorder, the violence, the terror, the war on the streets; when the earth seems to be chaos, say to yourself, 'Jesus died and rose again on purpose to save, and his salvation is already with us'.

When your father or your mother, your son or your daughter, your spouse or your friend are on their deathbed, and you are looking at them in the pain of parting, say 'We shall see each other again in the Kingdom; courage'.

This is what it means to believe in the resurrection.

But there is more.

Belief in the risen Christ means something else.

For Mother Teresa of Calcutta it means comforting the dying, and for you it means doing the same.

For Martin Luther King it meant facing death, and for you it means being unafraid to die for your brothers.

For Abbé Schultz, prior of Taizé, it means opening his convent to hope, and for you opening your house to hope.

Every departing missionary is an act of faith in the resurrection.

Every newly-opened leper-hospital is an act of faith in the resurrection.

Every peace treaty is an act of faith in the resurrection.

Every agreed commitment is an act of faith in the resurrection.

When you forgive your enemy
When you feed the hungry
When you defend the weak
you believe in the resurrection.
When you have the courage to marry
When you welcome the newly-born child
When you build your home
you believe in the resurrection.
When you wake at peace in the morning
When you sing to the rising sun
When you go to work with joy
you believe in the resurrection.

Belief in the resurrection means filling life with faith
it means believing in your brother,
it means fearlessness towards all.
Belief in the resurrection means knowing that God is your
father, Jesus your brother, and I, Mary, your sister and, if you
like,
your Mother.

9

PRAYING WITH MARY

Having attempted to say something about Mary of Nazareth herself, I would now like to say something about the prayers centred around her so that together we may pray to her.

Ever since the early days of Christianity, the most popular and simple form of Marian prayer has been to set aside a few days, at regular intervals, during which the faithful – either alone or in community – make themselves accessible to the action of the Holy Spirit invoked through Her who was so intimate with the Holy Spirit in her lifetime.

The choice of a period of nine days is the one that most commonly recurs, especially in the lives of simple people, that is to say people whose heads are not cluttered up with worldly matters, but who pray to live and try to get to the bottom of things.

This book and its meditations are arranged on a nine-day cycle, which I propose to you in all simplicity as my mother did to me. Whenever we were in trouble, she said: 'Let's make a novena to Our Lady'.

Our prayer has two lines of approach which I believe to be integral to authentic Marian devotion:
1) the biblical approach
2) the contemplative approach.

The biblical approach has as its aim to nourish the soul with God's word which becomes in its turn a source of theological inspiration and presents man in the true light of revelation, distancing him from pietistic distortions and sentimental superficiality.

The contemplative approach, on the other hand, takes biblical and theological nourishment for granted and brings man into the context of love which he expresses in simple repetitive formulas – such as a litany, such as the rosary, such as ejaculatory prayers. This type of prayer is almost always rhythmical and simple and repetitive.

At first glance this type of prayer might seem formal and immature and not too intelligent, yet for those who understand it the reverse is the case – it is mature and spontaneous prayer and endowed with the highest intelligence, which is to say the intelligence of the heart. If a bride says to her bridegroom, 'I love you', that is a good thing, but if she says it fifty times I do not think the bridegroom would complain or regard his bride as immature because she says the same thing over and over again. It is the property of love to be repetitive with simple rhythmical and warm words.

So to conclude: if you want to nourish your prayer with biblical texts, all right, do so; but if you feel that on returning from work it is better and more peaceful to take out your rosary and express yourself in rhythmic repetitive prayer, then that is what you should do.

And remember: if you manage to say the whole rosary free of distracting thoughts and are content simply to be at peace with the mother of Jesus, then be happy, for you are certainly under the action of the Spirit, and this is what matters when you pray.

So now you will consider the project for nine days of prayer.

In the suggestions below, the biblical approach gives ideas for Lauds, Vespers and Readings.

The contemplative approach follows with proposals for lines of thought and prayers of praise.

It is for you to choose in all simplicity, according to what is best suited to you personally.

In either case do not look for culture but for love.

That is always the truest and safest way to confront the divine rhythm of prayer.

DAY ONE: MARY, MY SISTER

Biblical Approach

Today's theme is what Mary has meant to me in my own life. Try to think about it – it may be easy for you, it may not. Read my first chapter here in this book where I describe my own experiences. Then you describe yours. Then try to pray.

Lauds	Psalm 8
	Psalm 13
	Moses' song (Exod. 15, 1/20).
Vespers	Psalm 4
	Psalm 11
	Hannah's song (1 Sam. 2,1/11).
Readings	Genesis 1
	Isaiah 59
	John 1.

Contemplative Approach

Let me tell you a new way of saying the rosary, the eastern way. Take your rosary and slip it through your fingers. On each bead say, 'Hail Mary!' and on every tenth bead alternate the ejaculation with the 'Hail Mary' said in full.

Or say on each bead: 'My Mother, I put my trust in you'.

Or: 'Let it be done to me according to your word'.

Throughout the day praise Mary like this:

O my one comfort,
divine dew, balm to my thirst,
rain falling from God upon the hardness of my heart,
shining light in the darkness of my soul,
guide on my journey,
support in my weakness,
clothing for my nakedness,
richness in my poverty,
healing for my wounds,
term of my tears and sighs,
freedom from my misfortunes,
relief from my sorrows,
freedom from my servitudes,
hope of my salvation . . .

So be it, O my Lady,
so be it, O my refuge,
my life and my help,
my protection and my glory,
my hope and my strength.

(St Germanus of Constantinople, 634–733.)*

*This prayer and the six that follow (except the Stabat Mater, the Magnificat, and 'Hail, Star of the sea') are taken from *Praises to the Madonna in the first Millenium of the Eastern and Western Churches* edited by Constante Berselli and Georges Charib (Pauline Publications, Rome, 1979).

DAY TWO: HAIL MARY

Biblical Approach

The theme is the annunciation.

I have tried to bring Mary as near as possible to our own lives. Annunciation means before anything God intervening in our lives: it is God with us. It also means a vocation, a calling, an invitation to accomplish our Exodus to freedom.

Mary teaches us courage and strength in faith.

Lauds	Psalm 16
	Psalm 18
	Moses' song (Deut. 32,1/43)
Vespers	Psalm 17
	Psalm 19
	Mary's Magnificat (Lk 1,46/55).
Readings	Exodus 17
	Colossians (all)
	Luke 1.

Contemplative Approach

The angel of the Lord brought the news to Mary
and she conceived through the work of the Holy Spirit

Behold I am the handmaid of the Lord
let it be done to me according to your word

And the Word was made flesh
and dwelt among us

$$\text{Hail Mary . . .}$$

Or:

Rejoice, O Mary, mother of the Lord, because you have received the good news.

Rejoice, O most holy of women, because all generations shall call you blessed.

Blessed are they who hear the word of God and keep it.

Rejoice, O Mary, lowly handmaid of the Lord, because you believed what he said.

Rejoice you who are filled with God's love, because every creature rejoices in you.

Blessed are they who hear the word of God and keep it.

Rejoice, O Mary, mother of the Messiah, because Christ is risen from the dead.

Rejoice, image of the Church, because Jesus has made you the mother of believers.

Blessed are they who hear the word of God and keep it.

Or:

With the Virgin Mary, mother of the Lord, our spirit magnifies the Lord and rejoices in Jesus our saviour.

Holy is the Lord for ever and ever!

With Mary, God's humble daughter, our heart sings and shouts: God is with us!

Holy is the Lord for ever and ever!

With Mary, the handmaid of the Lord, let us surrender our life to God and say: may his word be accomplished in us.

Holy is the Lord for ever and ever!

With Mary, our Lady clothed in the sun, let us give a sign to the world of the coming of the Lord.

Holy is the Lord for ever and ever!

With Mary, mother of Emmanuel, may we let the Word become flesh with us and bring us within its embrace.

Holy is the Lord for ever and ever!

Today you can say your rosary using what bits of the Angelus you like best, but do not forget this:

Behold the handmaid of the Lord
Let it be done to me according to your word.

At night praise Mary as follows:

Hail, canticle of the cherubim
    praise of angels.
Hail, peace and joy
    of the human race.
Hail, garden of delights,
    hail, O tree of life.

Hail, bastion of the faithful
  and harbour of the shipwrecked.
Hail, Adam's admonition
  hail, Eve's redemption.
Hail, fount of grace
  and of immortality.
Hail, holiest of temples
  hail, throne of the Lord.
Hail, O chaste one, who have crushed
  the head of the dragon
  and cast it into the abyss.
Hail, refuge of the afflicted
  hail, release from our curse.
Hail, O mother of Christ,
  son of the living God,
to whom belong glory and honour
  adoration and praise
  now and for ever and everywhere,
World without end, amen.

(St Ephraem Syrus, 306–373.)

DAY THREE: MY GOD, MY SON

Biblical Approach

God is born in Mary; God is born into our reality. All values have been reversed. The infinitely remote has become the infinitely near. Intimacy has replaced fear, trust has been born.

To be able to call God 'my son' – nobody could go further than that, and it shows that Mary had the courage to beget him in faith.

Lauds	Psalm 23
	Psalm 26
	Jonah's prayer (Jon. 2,1/10).
Vespers	Psalm 25
	Psalm 24
	Mary's Magnificat (Lk 1, 46/55).
Readings	Isaiah 35
	Psalm 24
	Luke 2.

Contemplative Approach

Today you will fill your empty minutes by saying your rosary in the 'eastern' way, using the formula: My God, my son. In this way you will see that faith really has the power to 'beget' God in your life, under the sign of your faith, your hope, your love.

Praise:
    Hail, mother of heavenly bliss,
    Hail, you who foster sublime joy within us,
    Hail, seat of the joy that saves,
    Hail, you who bestow eternal joy,
    Hail, O mystical centre of joy beyond words,
    Hail, O noblest home of joy beyond name,
    Hail, O blessed fount of infinite joy,
    Hail, O divine treasure of limitless joy,
    Hail, O shade-giving tree of life-giving joy,
    Hail, O mother of God, ever a virgin,
    Hail, O virgin intact after childbirth,
    Hail, most wonderful spectacle
    far beyond any other marvel.

Who could express your splendour?
Who could describe your mystery?
Who could proclaim your greatness?
You have adorned human nature,
You have surpassed the legions of angels,
You have surpassed every creature,
We acclaim you: Hail, full of grace!
                    (St Sophronius of Jerusalem, 560–638.)

DAY FOUR: THE CHAOS OF HISTORY

Biblical Approach

Today you will meditate on the weakness of a God who renounces his Godhead so as to enter into history and accept the consequences.

The massacre of the innocents epitomises the inexplicable chaos that Jesus accepts so as to save men, but it also proves that God's will is fulfilled over and beyond and in spite of man's arrogance.

Lauds	Psalm 28
	Psalm 30
	Habakkuk's prayer (Hab.3).
Vespers	Psalm 29
	Psalm 31
	The hymn of the three brothers (Dan. 3,29/68).
Readings	Jeremiah 9
	Hosea 2
	Luke 15.

Contemplative Approach

Today your ejaculatory prayer is: Everything is possible with God. And the praise:

My soul magnifies the Lord,
and my spirit rejoices in God my Saviour,
for he has regarded the low estate of his handmaiden.
For behold, henceforth all generations will call me blessed;
for he who is mighty has done great things for me
and holy is his name.
And his mercy is on those who fear him
from generation to generation.
He has shown strength with his arm,
he has scattered the proud in the imagination of their hearts,
he has put down the mighty from their thrones,
and exalted those of low degree;
he has filled the hungry with good things,
and the rich he has sent empty away.

He has helped his servant Israel,
in remembrance of his mercy,
as he spoke to our fathers,
to Abraham and to his posterity for ever.

(Lk 1, 46/55.)

DAY FIVE: NAZARETH

Biblical Approach

The meditation on Nazareth is a gold-mine and the closest to our ordinary lives.

Nazareth shows how to live in the world under the action of faith. Nazareth means God-with-us; it means the divinisation of simple things, such as work and human relationships. It means prayer twenty-four hours out of twenty-four.

Just see what depths this day enshrines:

Lauds	Psalm 33
	Psalm 37
	Song (Col. 2,6/11).
Vespers	Psalm 34
	Psalm 39
	Sirach (42,15/43,33).
Readings	Isaiah 53
	Ephesians (all)
	Luke 4.

Contemplative Approach

Today you could try to say the rosary. You know the traditional way to say it.

You announce the mystery and then you recite the Hail Mary ten times.

These are the five joyful mysteries:
1) the annunciation
2) the visitation
3) the nativity
4) the presentation of Jesus in the temple
5) the finding of Jesus in the temple.

For your praise say the following:
Hail, star of the sea,
glorious mother of God;
O blessed virgin Mary,
O wide-open gateway to heaven!

The angel sent from heaven
brings you a message from God.

By accepting it
you reverse Eve's destiny
and peace smiles on the world.

Break the chains of oppression,
offer your light to the blind,
remove evil from men,
ask for them all that is good.

May they know that you are our mother,
may you offer our prayers to Christ,
who made himself your son –
may he receive them with clemency.

Virgin most high, gentle and beloved,
free us from our faults,
make us humble and pure.
Grant us peaceful days,
watch over our journey
until we meet your son
merrily in heaven.

(Popular ninth-century hymn.)

DAY SIX: DO WHATEVER HE TELLS YOU

Biblical Approach

This is a meditation on commitment, on the apostolate, on service.

What is the apostolate? It is doing what Christ tells us to do – it is not action in a vacuum. Mary helps us to stay close to Jesus and to stir him with our prayer and force his hand with our love.

Lauds	Psalm 40
	Psalm 46
	Song (Is. 26,9/21).
Vespers	Psalm 42
	Psalm 47
	Mary's Magnificat (Lk 1,46/55).
Readings	Exodus 19/20
	Ezekiel 34
	John 15.

Contemplative Approach

Today you could say your rosary in the 'eastern' way with ejaculatory prayers on the apostolate. It is the theme of the day:
Father, send labourers to your harvest,
Father, save us, we are lost,
Father, may your kingdom come.

And for your evening hymn of praise:

O Mary, vastness of the heavens,
foundation of the earth,
depth of the oceans, light of the sun,
beauty of the moon,
splendour of the stars,
your womb contained God
whose majesty makes man tremble.
Your arms cradled the burning coal.
You held on your lap the lion
whose majesty is awesome.

Your hands touched
him who is untouchable
and the divine fire within him.
Your fingers are like the incandescent tongs
with which the prophet received the coal
of the heavenly offering.
You are the basket bearing this burning bread
and you are the cup of this wine.
O Mary, you bring forth in your womb
the fruit of the offering . . .
we most earnestly pray to you
that you may protect us from the ensnaring enemy
and that, just as the measure of water
is not divided from the wine,
so we may not separate ourselves from your son,
the lamb of salvation.

                              (Ethiopian anaphora.)

DAY SEVEN: THE DEATH OF JESUS

Biblical Approach

This meditation is basic for understanding Jesus's innermost thought. It discovers the face of the suffering Servant described by Isaiah and fulfilled by Christ. To understand this image is equivalent to entering into the good news of the Gospel, and vice versa.

Lauds	Psalm 22
	Psalm 51
	Zechariah's hymn (Lk 1,68/79).
Vespers	Psalm 55
	Psalm 57
	The servant's song (Is. 49,1/6).
Readings	Jeremiah 14/15
	Isaiah 53
	John 18/19.

Contemplative Approach

You could recite the rosary based on the sorrowful mysteries:
1) the agony in the garden
2) the scourging at the pillar
3) the crowning with thorns
4) the carrying of the cross
5) the crucifixion.

If you want to recite the rosary in the eastern way, then here are a couple of ejaculatory prayers:

Father, not my will but thine be done
My God, my God, why have you forsaken me?

And here is the *Stabat Mater*:

Stabat Mater

At the cross her station keeping
Stood the mournful Mother weeping
    Close to Jesus to the last:
Through her heart, his sorrow sharing
All his bitter anguish bearing,
    Now at length the sword has passed.

Oh, how sad and sore distressed
Was that Mother highly blest
  Of the sole-begotten One!
Christ above in torment hangs,
She beneath beholds the pangs
  Of her dying glorious Son.

Is there one who would not weep,
Whelmed in miseries so deep
  Christ's dear Mother to behold?
Can the human heart refrain
From partaking in her pain,
  In that Mother's pain untold?

Bruised, derided, cursed, defiled,
She beheld her tender Child
  All with bloody scourges rent;
For the sins of his own nation,
Saw him hang in desolation,
  Till his spirit forth he sent.

O thou Mother, fount of love,
Touch my spirit from above,
  Make my heart with thine accord:
Make me feel as thou hast felt,
Make my soul to glow and melt
  With the love of Christ my Lord.

Holy Mother, pierce me through,
In my heart each wound renew
  Of my Saviour crucified:
Let me share with thee his pain,
Who for all my sins was slain
  Who for me in torment died.

Let me mingle tears with thee,
Mourning him who mourned for me,
  All the days that I may live:
By the cross with thee to stay,
There with thee to weep and pray,
  Is all I ask of thee to give.

Virgin of all virgins blest!
Listen to my fond request:
　　Let me share thy grief divine;
Let me to my latest breath
In my body bear the death
　　Of that dying Son of thine.

Wounded with his every wound,
Steep my soul till it hath swooned
　　In his very blood away;
Be to me, O Virgin, nigh,
Lest in flames I burn and die
　　In his awful judgment day.

Christ, when thou shalt call me hence,
Be thy Mother my defence,
　　Be thy cross my victory;
While my body here decays
May my soul thy goodness praise,
　　Safe in paradise with thee.

(Ascribed to Jacopone da Todi – 13th century–
in the traditional translation by Rev. E. Caswall.)

DAY EIGHT: HE IS RISEN

Biblical Approach

What does it mean to believe that Christ rose from the dead?
  Mary says it all.
  Let us get away from rhetoric and emotionalism and even
from fideism and go straight into the dynamics of faith, hope
and charity – the only territory where Jesus's resurrection is
daily fulfilled.

Lauds	Psalm 62
	Psalm 68
	Song (Ezek. 37,1/15).
Vespers	Psalm 66
	Psalm 84
	Song (Apoc. 5,1/13).
Readings	Jonah (all)
	Apocalypse 21/22
	Luke 24.

Contemplative Approach

If you say your rosary in the eastern way today, use as
ejaculatory prayers:

  Christ is risen
  he is risen indeed
and say them until your mouth goes dry. And at night praise
Mary like this:

  O Virgin, out of you,
  as from an uncleft mountain,
  Christ came forth, the corner stone
  uniting separate natures.
  For this we rejoice
  and glorify you, O mother of God!

  Come, let us celebrate
  with pure heart and temperate mind
  the King's daughter,
  the splendour of the Church,
  brighter than gold,
  let us glorify her!

Hail! and rejoice O bride of the great King,
you who splendidly reflect
the beauty of your spouse
and exclaim with your people,
O Giver of life!
We glorify you!

O Saviour, grant your heavenly help
to your Church;
she acknowledges no other God
no other liberator, save you,
who gave your life for her
and she glorifies you in gratitude.

Listen to the supplications of your people
O virgin mother of God,
and intercede without pause with your son,
so that you may free us, who praise you,
from peril and temptation.
You are indeed our ambassadress
and our hope.

(St Andrew of Crete, 660–740.)

DAY NINE: WITH MARY

Biblical Approach

Lauds
Psalm 89
Psalm 103
The heavenly Jerusalem (Apoc. 21).

Vespers
Psalm 91
Psalm 104
Mary's Magnificat (Lk 1,46/55).

Readings
Isaiah 42
Philippians (all)
John 17.

Contemplative Approach

Our short nine-day retreat, made in the company of Mary, is now drawing to a close.

You can choose, or, better, make up for yourself, your basic ejaculatory prayer, your 'secret', which from now on you will say as your expression of love in your meetings with Him. This will help you to reach a level of 'continuous prayer'.

At night say the following:

Hail, O full of grace, the Lord is with you!
    Hail, O longed-for object of our delight!
Hail, O source of the Church's rejoicing!
    Hail, O name redolent of fragrance!
Hail, O countenance radiant with God and aglow with beauty!
    Hail, O repository of everything revered!
Hail, O soft fleece, health-giving and spiritual!
    Hail, O fairest mother of dawning light!
Hail, O unblemished mother of holiness!
    Hail, O gushing spring of living water!
Hail, O bright new mother, shaper of the new birth!
Hail, O mother inexplicable and full of mystery!
    Hail, O alabaster vase
    of the ointment of sanctification!
Hail, you who show the value of virginity!
    Hail, O little space, that held within it
Him whom the world cannot contain!
                    (Theodotus, bishop of Ancyra, d. 445.)

The Rosary

As the rosary has played such an important part in the novena, I wish to say something more about it.

First, as I have already hinted, for anyone unacquainted with the spiritual life the rosary can seem a useless and rhetorical form of prayer.

But for the person who is 'spiritual', for the person who has advanced along the path of prayer, the rosary is the simplest method of helping him to live prayer in a down-to-earth and sustained way.

I would go so far as to say that the person who loves this type of prayer, and who feels at ease in reciting the rosary, is a contemplative, or certainly on the road to contemplation.

So beware of speaking ill of things you do not know about!

The rosary is a universal way of prayer – in fact it is to be found in all the revealed religions.

I shall indicate three ways in which it can be used during our novena.

The Marian rosary – that is to say, our rosary

This consists of fifty beads divided into five groups of ten which are separated from each other by one larger bead. It is a genuine little office of Our Lady and a straightforward way of helping people to pray. In the Catholic tradition it has played a basic part. For many of the poor it has been their only support in sustaining their faith in cruelly adverse times.

The rosary is an attempt to unite a charted meditation on the life of the Virgin with the repetitive and litany-like recitation of the Hail Mary – and all within the span of fifteen minutes.

The meditation chart is very simple. It consists of:

Mary's joy,

Mary's sorrow,

Mary's glory,

and is based on five themes called mysteries – the term is medieval when sacred plays were called mystery plays.

In order to avoid monotony the arrangement goes like this:

Monday } Mary's joy
Thursday } the joyful mysteries

Tuesday } Mary's sorrow
Friday } the sorrowful mysteries

Wednesday	Mary's glory
Saturday	the glorious mysteries
Sunday	

The joyful mysteries and the sorrowful mysteries have already been listed (see pp. 72 and 76) so here are the glorious mysteries:

1) the resurrection
2) the ascension
3) the descent of the Holy Ghost on the apostles
4) the assumption
5) the crowning of Mary in heaven.

The Byzantine rosary

We call it 'rosary' so as to understand each other, but in fact in the Byzantine liturgy it is called *Cotki* and in Russian *Comvolojan*.

It is a rosary made of wool with one hundred beads which you slip through your fingers while saying on each bead:

'Lord Jesus Christ
Son of the living God
have mercy on me, a sinner.'

It has the same origin as the famous Jesus prayer of the *Russian Pilgrim*:

'Lord have mercy
I am a sinner!'

Repeating this prayer over and over again is a very useful way of 'putting to sleep' both *thought* and *imagination*.

Just as a mother puts her baby to sleep by rocking it, so the rhythm and monotony of repetition placate and quieten those two uncontrollable entities which are always lying in wait to distract us from our prayer.

The Islamic rosary (Subha)

This is unquestionably the simplest and most perfect form of this prayer — it is the prayer of the desert, of long treks, of adoration and prolonged praise.

This rosary is made up of 99 beads (corresponding to the 99 praises of God) and you slip it through your fingers while saying just one invocation selected from the 99.

It is a truly astonishing fount of prayer.

No-one in love with God can ever tire of repeating it.

When you travel in Islamic countries you will certainly see 'believers' walking along with the rosary in their hands, and, as they slip the beads through their fingers, their lips will murmur:

'My God, how great you are'

or

'God, you are merciful.'

Often the chosen exclamation is a personal 'secret'.

For instance, I have never managed to get anyone, even a friend, to tell me what exclamatory phrase he has chosen for his prayer.

However, as I am less secretive, I shall tell you mine. It is:

'My God I love you

have mercy on me',

and I would wager that no bride in the world has said 'I love you' to her husband oftener than I have said it.

Here are the 99 praises of God:*

Benefactor	He who opens
Merciful	He who shuts
King	Prophet
Beauty	Attentive
Peace	Judge
Faithful	Just
Defender	Subtle
Mighty	Observer
Healer	Clement
Great	Magnanimous
Fruitful	Pleasing
Creator	Glorified
Vigilant	Magnificent
Indulgent	Guardian
Master	Bestower
Giver	Providence
Dispenser	Majestic
Conqueror	Generous
Knowledge	Sentinel
He who sees	Protector

*These praises are expressed repetitively and in a variety of parts of speech, possibly the result of double translation from the original language. (Tr).

He who answers
Wise
Splendid
Most loving
He who lowers
He who raises
He who bestows dignity
He who takes away
Invincible
Holy
Worthy of all praise
Omniscient
Prince
Resurrection
Master of death
Living
Abundant
New
Immutable
Unique
Eternal
Goodness
Charity
Prudent
He who produces
He who anticipates
First
Last
Revealed
Hidden

Most excellent
Omnipotent
Witness
Truth
Strong
Righteous
Forgiveness
Justice
Good
Lovable
Kingdom
Lord of majesty
Lord of generosity
Equitable
He who unites
Sufficient
Rich
He who holds goods
He who divides them
He who distributes them
Light
Compassionate
Glorious
Universal
Guide
Perfect
Sublime
Patient
Sweetness

The hundredth praise is a secret, and God reveals it personally to whomsoever asks him.

The Author

Carlo Carretto, born in 1910, was from 1946 to 1952 President of Catholic Action in Italy. In 1954 he entered the order of the Little Brothers of Jesus, inspired by Charles de Foucauld, and he lives now a life of prayer and meditation and writing in one of the communities of the Little Brothers in Spello, near Assisi. His books which have been translated into English include *The God Who Comes, Letters from the Desert, In Search of Beyond, Love is for Living* and *The Desert in the City*.